Baby Bear's Real Name

Story by Beverley Randell   Illustrations by Isabel Lowe

One cold morning,
Father Bear and Baby Bear
went down to the river.

Baby Bear looked at the water.
He saw something move.
Was it a fish?
He jumped in to catch it.

Baby Bear came out of the river with a big fish in his arms.

"Look!" he said.
"I can catch fish all by myself."

"You are a clever little bear," said Father Bear.

Baby Bear looked at Father Bear.
"But I'm **not** little!" he said.
"I'm a big bear now!"

"Yes," said Father Bear.
"You are getting taller every day!"

That night Baby Bear said,

"It's my birthday tomorrow.

I'm not a baby any more.

I don't like being called Baby Bear!

I want a **real** name."

"You do have a real name,"
said Mother Bear.

"What is it?" said Baby Bear.
"What is my real name?"

"Your name is **Hector**,"
said Father Bear.

"Your grandfather
was called Hector, too,"
said Father Bear.

"Grandfather was very brave,"
said Mother Bear.
"He loved climbing great mountains.
Here is a photo of him."

Baby Bear smiled.

"Hector!" he said. "Hector Bear!

I **like** that name.

One day I'm going

to climb great mountains, too.

I want to be

as brave as my grandfather."

The next day,

Mother Bear made a birthday cake.

She made it look like a mountain!

And the name on the cake was...